TIM CHESTER

Preparing for
BAPTISM

Exploring what the Bible says
about baptism

Preparing for Baptism
Exploring what the Bible says about baptism
© The Good Book Company 2016. Reprinted 2017, 2020, 2021.

Published by:
The Good Book Company

thegoodbook.com | thegoodbook.co.uk
thegoodbook.com.au | thegoodbook.co.nz | thegoodbook.co.in

Unless indicated, all Scripture references are taken from the Holy Bible, New International Version. Copyright © 2011 Biblica, Inc. Used by permission.

All rights reserved. Except as may be permitted by the Copyright Act, no part of this publication may be reproduced in any form or by any means without prior permission from the publisher.

ISBN: 9781784980702 | Printed in Turkey

Design by Ben Woodcraft

Contents

Introduction 5

Session 1: Baptism is a sign that
we have a new hope........................ 7

Session 2: Baptism is a sign that
we have a new family....................13

Session 3: Baptism is a sign that
we have a new life..........................21

Introduction

"What shall we do?" This is what people asked the apostle Peter when he had finished preaching about Jesus on the day of Pentecost.

> Peter replied, "Repent and be baptised, every one of you, in the name of Jesus Christ for the forgiveness of your sins. And you will receive the gift of the Holy Spirit. 39 The promise is for you and your children and for all who are far off—for all whom the Lord our God will call."
>
> **(Acts 2 v 38-39)**

Perhaps you feel God calling you to be a Christian. Perhaps someone has told you about Jesus and you want to know what to do next. Perhaps you grew up in a Christian home, but now you want to express your own personal faith. Peter says, "Repent and be baptised".

Peter also says, "The promise is for you and your children". Maybe your parents had you baptised when you were a child because they wanted to express God's promise of salvation to you. And now perhaps you're wondering what that means.

We're going to look at how baptism shows us what it means to be a Christian.

Note for Leaders
A free downloadable leader's guide is available to use with this study guide.

You can find it at:
www.thegoodbook.co.uk/preparing-for-baptism-leaders-guide (UK & Europe)
www.thegoodbook.com/preparing-for-baptism-leaders-guide (N. America)
www.thegoodbook.com.au/preparing-for-baptism-leaders-guide (Australia)
www.thegoodbook.co.nz/preparing-for-baptism-leaders-guide (New Zealand).

session 1

Baptism is a sign that we have a new hope

About this passage
This extract is from one of the four accounts in the Bible of the life of Jesus. John the Baptist was a prophet appointed by God to prepare for the coming of Jesus.

Mark 1 v 4-11

And so John the Baptist appeared in the wilderness, preaching a baptism of repentance for the forgiveness of sins. [5] The whole Judean countryside and all the people of Jerusalem went out to him. Confessing their sins, they were baptised by him in the River Jordan. [6] John wore clothing made of camel's hair, with a leather belt round his waist, and he ate locusts and wild honey. [7] And this was his message: "After me comes the one more powerful than I, the straps of whose sandals I am not worthy to stoop down and untie. [8] I baptise you with water, but he will baptise you with the Holy Spirit."
[9] At that time Jesus came from Nazareth in Galilee and was baptised by John in the Jordan. [10] Just as Jesus was coming up out of the water, he saw heaven being torn open and the Spirit descending on him like a dove. [11] And a voice came from heaven: "You are my Son, whom I love; with you I am well pleased."

1. Look at verses 4-5. What was the significance of the baptism John was offering?

_____

_____

Jesus lived a perfect life, so he didn't need to confess any sins or have any sins forgiven. So, when he was baptised, he wasn't identifying himself *as* a sinner. Instead he was identifying himself *with* sinners.

2. Look at verse 11. What was God the Father's verdict on Jesus?

_____

_____

About this passage
James and John were two of Jesus' disciples. Just before this conversation Jesus had predicted that he would soon be arrested and executed, and then rise from the dead.

> **Mark 10 v 35-38**
> Then James and John, the sons of Zebedee, came to [Jesus]. "Teacher," they said, "we want you to do for us whatever we ask."
> ³⁶ "What do you want me to do for you?" he asked.
> ³⁷ They replied, "Let one of us sit at your right and the other at your left in your glory."
> ³⁸ "You don't know what you are asking," Jesus said. "Can you drink the cup I drink or be baptised with the baptism I am baptised with?"

Jesus is talking about his death, using two pictures: "baptism" and "the cup".

- **Baptism:** In the Old Testament, water was sometimes a sign of God's judgment. God judged the world at the time of Noah with a flood (Genesis 6 v 9 – 8 v 22). He destroyed the Egyptian army in the waters of the Red Sea (Exodus 14).
- **The cup:** Drinking the cup of God's wrath is another picture of judgment in the Old Testament (for example, Jeremiah 25 v 15-16).

3. What is Jesus saying about the meaning of his baptism by John?

4. What is Jesus saying about the meaning of his death?

Baptism is like a wedding

In his baptism Jesus identified with us (he was willing to be treated like a sinner, despite being sinless). And when we put our faith in Jesus, God identifies us with Jesus. We're united to Jesus and this is what is displayed and sealed in baptism. So baptism is like a wedding. Imagine a poor slave girl marrying a prince: he takes her debts and covers them; she receives his status. Jesus lived the life we should have lived and died the death that we deserve to die.

About this passage
One of the main leaders among the first Christians was the apostle Paul. This extract is from a letter he wrote to a church in Ephesus (in modern-day Turkey).

> **Ephesians 2 v 8-10**
>
> For it is by grace you have been saved, through faith—and this is not from yourselves, it is the gift of God— ⁹ not by works, so that no one can boast. ¹⁰ For we are God's handiwork, created in Christ Jesus to do good works, which God prepared in advance for us to do.

5. What do you need to do to be saved from God's judgment?

6. How would you put these verses in your own words?

7. Look again at Mark 1 v 11 (p7). What is God's verdict on you if you are united to Jesus, do you think?

1 Peter 3 v 21 says baptism is "the pledge of a clear conscience towards God. It saves you by the resurrection of Jesus Christ." Baptism itself doesn't save us. It's not a magical act. We're saved by the death and resurrection of Jesus Christ. Baptism is this promise to us expressed in physical form. It's like a wedding ring. A husband gives a wedding ring as a sign of his love and commitment. Baptism is a sign of Christ's love and commitment to us.

8. Are you confident that God will give you eternal life? What gives you this confidence? Or what stops you having this confidence?

_____

_____

_____

_____

9. Do you have any questions about Jesus and the hope that he offers?

_____

_____

_____

_____

session
2

Baptism is a sign that we have a new family

About this passage
This extract is from a letter by the apostle Paul to a church in Galatia (in modern-day Turkey). Some people in Galatia were saying that faith in Jesus Christ was not enough. They said people also needed to keep the Jewish law if they wanted to be part of God's people. This extract is Paul's response to this false claim. Abraham was the father of the Jewish nation, so "Abraham's seed" is another way of referring to God's true people.

Galatians 3 v 26 – 4 v 7
So in Christ Jesus you are all children of God through faith, [27] for all of you who were baptised into Christ have clothed yourselves with Christ. [28] There is neither Jew nor Gentile, neither slave nor free, nor is there male and female, for you are all one in Christ Jesus. [29] If you belong to Christ, then you are Abraham's seed, and heirs according to the promise.
4 What I am saying is that as long as an heir is under age, he is no different from a slave, although he owns the whole estate. [2] The heir is subject to guardians and trustees until the time set by his father. [3] So also, when we were under age, we were in slavery under the elemental spiritual forces of the world. [4] But when the set time had fully come, God sent his Son, born of a woman, born under the law, [5] to redeem those under the law, that we might receive adoption to sonship.
[6] Because you are his sons, God sent the Spirit of his Son into our hearts, the Spirit who calls out, "*Abba*, Father." [7] So you are no longer a slave, but God's child; and since you are his child, God has made you also an heir.

1. Look at 3 v 26-27. How do you become part of God's family?

2. Look at verse 28. Who can be part of God's family?

Galatians 4 v 1-5 tells us that, before the coming of Jesus, God's people, Israel, were like under-age children without the full rights of heirs. But Jesus has come to set us free so we can live as God's children like true heirs.

3. Look at 4 v 6-7. Why does God give us the Holy Spirit?

4. What are some of the benefits of being a child of God, do you think?

_____

_____

_____

_____

God has given us "the Spirit *of his Son*" so we can share the experience of his Son. We are loved with the same love that God the Father has for his own Son.

About this passage
This extract is from a letter by the apostle Paul to a church in the Greek city of Corinth. The church had a number of problems including deep divisions.

---

1 Corinthians 12 v 12-26

Just as a body, though one, has many parts, but all its many parts form one body, so it is with Christ. [13] For we were all baptised by one Spirit so as to form one body—whether Jews or Gentiles, slave or free—and we were all given the one Spirit to drink. [14] And so the body is not made up of one part but of many.

[15] Now if the foot should say, "Because I am not a hand, I do not belong to the body," it would not for that reason stop being part of the body. [16] And if the ear should say, "Because I am not an eye, I do not belong to the body," it would not for that reason stop being part of the body. [17] If the whole body were an eye, where would the sense of hearing be? If the whole body were an ear, where would the sense of smell be? [18] But in fact God has placed the parts in the body, every one of them, just as he wanted them to be. [19] If they were all one part, where would the body be? [20] As it is, there are many parts, but one body.

[21] The eye cannot say to the hand, "I don't need you!" And the head cannot say to the feet, "I don't need you!" [22] On the contrary, those parts of the body that seem to be weaker are indispensable, [23] and the parts that we think are less honourable we treat with special honour.

> And the parts that are unpresentable are treated with special modesty, [24] while our presentable parts need no special treatment. But God has put the body together, giving greater honour to the parts that lacked it, [25] so that there should be no division in the body, but that its parts should have equal concern for each other. [26] If one part suffers, every part suffers with it; if one part is honoured, every part rejoices with it.

We're baptised into Christ and that means we're baptised into Christ's body, the church. The church is the family of God. And that means other Christians become our brothers and sisters.

5. How do verses 15-20 speak to someone who feels they have nothing to contribute to their church?

6. How do verses 21-25 speak to someone who feels they don't need their church?

7. Look at verse 26. How have you seen Christians identifying with one another and caring for one another?

_____

_____

_____

8. What does it mean for you to be committed to your church?

_____

_____

_____

Baptism is a naming ceremony

One of the last things Jesus said on earth was this: "Therefore go and make disciples of all nations, *baptising them in the name* of the Father and of the Son and of the Holy Spirit." Baptism is a naming ceremony. At baptism we receive the name of the Father, Son and Holy Spirit. We become part of God's family.

About this passage

This extract is from one of the four accounts in the Bible of the life of Jesus. Jesus said these words after his resurrection and before his ascension into heaven.

Matthew 28 v 18-20

Then Jesus came to [the disciples] and said, "All authority in heaven and on earth has been given to me. [19] Therefore go and make disciples of all nations, baptising them in the name of the Father and of the Son and of the Holy Spirit, [20] and teaching them to obey everything I have commanded you. And surely I am with you always, to the very end of the age."

9. What does Jesus tell us to do?

_____

_____

_____

10. Why does Jesus tell us to do this, do you think?

_____

_____

_____

11. What does it mean for you to be committed to the mission of your church?

_____

_____

_____

_____

Baptism is a sign that we have a new life

About this passage
This extract is from a letter by the apostle Paul to a church in Rome. Paul's main theme is God's grace: God's kindness to people who deserve his condemnation. Some people said this means it doesn't matter if we sin. This extract is Paul's response to this false claim.

Romans 6 v 1-14

What shall we say, then? Shall we go on sinning, so that grace may increase? ² By no means! We are those who have died to sin; how can we live in it any longer? ³ Or don't you know that all of us who were baptised into Christ Jesus were baptised into his death? ⁴ We were therefore buried with him through baptism into death in order that, just as Christ was raised from the dead through the glory of the Father, we too may live a new life.

⁵ For if we have been united with him in a death like his, we will certainly also be united with him in a resurrection like his. ⁶ For we know that our old self was crucified with him so that the body ruled by sin might be done away with, that we should no longer be slaves to sin— ⁷ because anyone who has died has been set free from sin.

⁸ Now if we died with Christ, we believe that we will also live with him. ⁹ For we know that since Christ was raised from the dead, he cannot die again; death no longer has mastery over him. ¹⁰ The death he died, he died to sin once for all; but the life he lives, he lives to God.

¹¹ In the same way, count yourselves dead to sin but alive to God in Christ Jesus. ¹² Therefore do not let sin reign in your mortal body so that you obey its evil desires. ¹³ Do not offer any part of yourself to

> sin as an instrument of wickedness, but rather offer yourselves to God as those who have been brought from death to life; and offer every part of yourself to him as an instrument of righteousness. [14] For sin shall no longer be your master, because you are not under the law, but under grace.

1. "Why should I stop sinning since God promises to forgive me?" How would you answer this question?

2. What do verses 3-4 say about baptism?

Baptism is like a funeral

Becoming a Christian is more than a change of opinions or priorities. Our old self dies and a new self is born. So baptism is like a funeral. As the water covers us, our old self is symbolically buried with Jesus. Because we are united with Christ by faith, his crucifixion is our death and his resurrection is our new life.

3. What do verses 5-10 say about the rule of sin and the mastery of death?

_____

_____

_____

_____

We used to have a deep-seated bias against God that meant we would never and could never live for him. We were controlled by our sin, selfishness and pride. The result was death—a fate we could not avoid. But God had a radical solution. He caused us to die with Christ so now sin and death no longer control us. And then he gave us a new life.

4. Look at verses 11-14. How are we to live now?

_____

_____

_____

_____

About this passage
Just before this extract, the followers of Jesus have grasped that he is God's promised King, and Jesus has predicted his death. Now he tells them what it means to follow him. "The Son of Man" was the main way in which Jesus referred to himself.

Mark 8 v 34-38

Then [Jesus] called the crowd to him along with his disciples and said: "Whoever wants to be my disciple must deny themselves and take up their cross and follow me. ³⁵ For whoever wants to save their life will lose it, but whoever loses their life for me and for the gospel will save it. ³⁶ What good is it for someone to gain the whole world, yet forfeit their

> soul? ³⁷ Or what can anyone give in exchange for their soul? ³⁸ If anyone is ashamed of me and my words in this adulterous and sinful generation, the Son of Man will be ashamed of them when he comes in his Father's glory with the holy angels."

5. How does Jesus describe what it means to follow him?

6. What does this look like for you?

7. When might you be ashamed of Jesus and his words?

8. What reasons does Jesus give for following him?

Mark 1 v 4, 7-8

And so John the Baptist appeared in the wilderness, preaching a baptism of repentance for the forgiveness of sins ... ⁷ And this was his message: "After me comes the one more powerful than I, the straps of whose sandals I am not worthy to stoop down and untie. ⁸ I baptise you with water, but he will baptise you with the Holy Spirit."

---

9. Water baptism is an outward sign. What, does John say, is the inner reality to which baptism points?

Jesus cancels the penalty of sin and breaks the power of sin. He also gives us the Holy Spirit to help us. The Holy Spirit gives us a new desire to please God, and he reassures us of God's love.

Jesus gives us other things to help us live as his people.

The Bible

God is not silent. He has revealed himself in his Son, Jesus. The Bible is the Spirit-inspired record of that revelation. The Spirit ensures the Bible is without error, so we can trust what it says. The Bible tells us about who Jesus is, what he has done and how we should follow him. We live under its authority because it's God's word. And it's not just a word from long ago. Through the Holy Spirit, Jesus speaks to us today through the Bible. In the Bible we hear his voice.

Prayer

God saved us so that we can enjoy a relationship with him. We hear his voice in the Bible and we speak to him in prayer. In prayer we praise him for his kindness and ask him for his help. People are sometimes intimidated by prayer, but it's not complicated. Jesus says prayer is like a child talking to their father. All we need in order to pray is the belief that God is our Father—and the Spirit gives this to us. We pray to God the Father, confident that he is powerful enough to help and loving enough to care.

The church

God has given us the church to help us. The church gathers:

- to hear God's word being taught.

- to pray together for his help.

- to remind one another of God's goodness and glory.

But the church is not just a meeting. We're a family, and so we share our lives together, look after one another and remind one another of Jesus.

10. Do you have any questions about the Bible, prayer or the church?

> **Being baptised**
>
> If you're going to be baptised, make sure you discuss what will happen. Some churches baptise people by immersing them in water. Other churches pour or sprinkle water over people. You may need to bring a towel and a change of clothing. Make sure you avoid light clothing that might become see-through when wet.

What will you be expected to say?

_____

_____

_____

What will you be expected to do?

_____

_____

_____

Is there anyone you could invite who doesn't normally come to your church?

_____

_____

_____

Help to grow in the Christian life

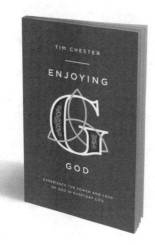

Enjoying God
Tim Chester

What exactly does a personal relationship with God look like, and how is it even possible? This seminal work by Tim Chester shows us how we can enjoy God in every moment of every day. He explores how the Father, the Son and the Spirit relate to us in our day-to-day lives, and how to respond.

You Can Really Grow
John Hindley

The Christian life can be about thriving, not merely surviving. Discover what Christian growth actually is, and how to enjoy it.

Get into a good habit

Explore Bible-reading notes

Daily readings to help you understand the message and challenge of God's word.

- **Lets the Bible set the agenda.**
- **Gets you looking at the text for yourself.**
- **Application that gets to the heart.**

Explore App

Download for free at the App Store or Google Play. Search 'Explore Bible'. Then buy content from within the app.

BIBLICAL | RELEVANT | ACCESSIBLE

At The Good Book Company, we are dedicated to helping Christians and local churches grow. We believe that God's growth process always starts with hearing clearly what he has said to us through his timeless word—the Bible.

Ever since we opened our doors in 1991, we have been striving to produce Bible-based resources that bring glory to God. We have grown to become an international provider of user-friendly resources to the Christian community, with believers of all backgrounds and denominations using our books, Bible studies, devotionals, evangelistic resources, and DVD-based courses.

We want to equip ordinary Christians to live for Christ day by day, and churches to grow in their knowledge of God, their love for one another, and the effectiveness of their outreach.

Call us for a discussion of your needs or visit one of our local websites for more information on the resources and services we provide.

Your friends at The Good Book Company

thegoodbook.com | thegoodbook.co.uk
thegoodbook.com.au | thegoodbook.co.nz
thegoodbook.co.in